No Chronology

KAREN FISH

No Chronology

THE UNIVERSITY OF CHICAGO PRESS

Chicago and London

The University of Chicago Press, Chicago 60637
The University of Chicago Press, Ltd., London
© 2021 by The University of Chicago
Published 2021
Printed in the United States of America

30 29 28 27 26 25 24 23 22 21   1 2 3 4 5

ISBN-13: 978-0-226-76897-7 (paper)
ISBN-13: 978-0-226-76902-8 (e-book)
DOI: https://doi.org/10.7208/chicago/9780226769028.001.0001

Library of Congress Cataloging-in-Publication Data

Names: Fish, Karen, 1959- author.
Title: No chronology / Karen Fish.
Other titles: Phoenix poets.
Description: Chicago : University of Chicago Press, 2021. | Series: Phoenix
    poets
Identifiers: LCCN 2020032202 | ISBN 9780226768977 (paperback) | ISBN
    9780226769028 (ebook)
Classification: LCC PS3556.I77 N6 2021 | DDC 811/.54—dc23
LC record available at https://lccn.loc.gov/2020032202

♾ This paper meets the requirements of ANSI/NISO Z39.48-1992
(Permanence of Paper).

CONTENTS

*

ACKNOWLEDGMENTS

Some of these poems have been published in the following magazines, to whose editors grateful acknowledgment is made:

> *Denver Quarterly*: "Do You Believe in the Afterlife?" and "The Dream"
> *DoubleTake*: "Caravaggio's *The Calling of St. Matthew*"
> *New Republic*: "Seen from Far Away"
> *Ploughshares*: "Another Republic"
> *Poetry*: "The Cistern," "Flames Behind Your Head," and "Driving in Spring"
> *Slate*: "The Round-Up"

* * *

FIRST TEACHER

My beauty was in my sadness.
Sometimes, I think I was chosen simply because
of where I happened to be standing. A girl out in the open,
before rock cliffs not realizing everyone could tell, read
the abandonment clearly as a smile on my face.

But despite the odd adult humility, how I stood
had ambition. I stood at the bottom of the steep
path, the bottom of the sheer face of
the cliffs before the old sea. The sea tossed
under the high saturation and low brilliance
of marine light. It was like a painting.

The teacher read aloud. The girl I was read aloud.
The value of critique, I understood immediately,
took to the way a swimmer finds even farther
distances to manage. The attention, his attention,
was very much like a surveillance.
The generosity floated large and bright
in the rigor. His generosity was the sun. And
the rigor was the muscle of the sky and
sea holding the light in place to frame the brightness.

Retrospectively, it is very clear, it all had to do with
what he hadn't managed himself. I was a surrogate.
It is often this way—a girl in a dress and sandals,

a man past his prime, after a return from Yugoslavia,
Turkey. He was a man who had traveled,
was fluent in many languages.
Disappointment is a rugged country.

It ended up being all about solitude.
There was the stripped room, shuttered
windows, and after the day's tutorial,
the ancient scent of sea,
empty walking,
then, the swimming,
swimming out too far.

ARS POETICA

My mother drowned off the coast, the deep water too swift and cold.

The trees blowing at dusk, a loud tide coming in.

My mother's mother loved story, with a modest red dot
birthmark between her small breasts, centered in the V-neck
of the full-flare dress with the regimental tulips—she points
to the tiny ruby dot, tells me when we are transformed, if she
at some point is wholly unrecognizable—I can know her
by that, the mark near her heart.

My grandfather asks how I'll know him in heaven.
Will he be old, or as he knows himself essentially:
someone with good humor, in a prime I've never seen; tall,
in baggy trousers and white cotton shirt, eating oysters
and drinking beer at his parents' summer place,
the red setter unspooling fast into the orchard through
the gritty collapse of sunlight on deer scent and
every lengthening shadow, brightly breathless?
My grandfather wants to know,
will I be a girl and he a grandfather
in the afterlife? Or might we somehow
transcend present form? What do I think?

I was ten, in fifth grade, failing fractions.
In the abstract, I couldn't break anything down.
I couldn't go beyond the whole number.

We walked, collected pine cones, looked at gardens, considered—
drove old cemeteries. I stayed up late learning card games,
bet nickels, was encouraged to strategize, imagine
a future several steps forward, know
what the opponent might be considering.
I was coaxed to speculate different outcomes, know moves.

Past tense, present tense, first person narration,
third person omniscient. . . .

A story could be prompted by a stranger coming to town
or an unwanted relative appearing unannounced—
complication, crisis, climax, the consequences, then
denouncement—
which was resolution.

And then I loved it—analogy, metaphor.
One could lie to tell the truth.

In their story, my grandmother was in nursing school,
just after the turn of the century, having escaped
a mining town, factory work where she cut threads.
My grandfather was home for the summer after
clerking for the court and law school.
When my grandfather and his friends came upon
the cluster of student nurses outside the fair,
he said, "I'm only going if I get the black-haired one."
She hadn't even spoken.

In the painting of the crucifixion, Christ hangs by his palms
over the outcropping of rock. The painting is in the back
of the church in the dimly lit corner above a pile of extra hymnals.
It was my understanding it was there to illustrate forgiveness.

I didn't yet know to forgive meant simply
to let go, to accept what is—

that the Roman soldiers were oblivious, Pilate a mundane
government official. The sky was that odd green
armature of clouds. Nothing more—parishioners
ran to their cars covering their heads with church bulletins,
the occasional newspaper under the swords of lightning.
It's a hunched and funny stooped run the believers do
as the sky opens.

It's charged; if the sudden downpour had a taste of metal,
the smell—something scorched.

ORPHAN

Like a fairy tale, it's never considered; instead,
it is known by rote, a sort of refrain, a child's song,
like climbing stairs, buttoning a shirt, maybe even
turning when one's name is called.
I was the chosen one.

The "story" is told and retold, small things embellished:
the mother's beauty, selflessness, rough circumstances but
the cord utilitarian, simplistic. Mysterious, not
that I ever thought it particularly mysterious.

So much not to know—mystery was the least of it.
Mystery implies tone, something to figure out,
characters, motives, plot, theater.
There was no plot, there were no retrievable characters.
Nothing—when people mentioned the child as lucky, was lucky—
I always knew I wasn't theirs.

If thought about, it was a momentary thing,
a witch handing a child out
of a thicket, thorns of dark woods.
The story relinquished.

The child relinquished.
Wanting to know more—relinquished.
The understanding was implied—there are
things to give up *always*—
always things to declare, then, give up.

One might be asked for the dearest thing, always.

A witch handing a child to a passerby. *Yes,*
we will take the baby. Yes. In my mind it was a parable
with old-world simplicity, a confusion of bells, smoke, peril,
understanding there is always a middleman—
even in a fairy tale—who wipes the backstory away,

off the page, and that not knowing
is a sort of geography, terrain to hike forever after,
after that. Not knowing, not just the white space,
not just about no symbolism.
Not knowing, atmospheric,

a scenic overlook, the Alps.
Breadcrumbs leading backward eaten by birds, really.
Real birds with appetite.

ALIBI

I knew nothing about anything: school, dreams, tornados,
strangers, smoke-filled bars, silent, oblivious mothers,

the teenage girls across the street, swaying and sashaying
through the late afternoons with transistor radios,

leaning in, in through rolled-down windows of the parked cars
of visiting boys. I worried in my not-knowing of iron lungs,

bursting appendix, accidental curse words,
sudden illness, all manners of medical procedures,

the gas chamber, the French Kiss. I knew nothing
about majorettes, although I tossed a baton in the warm

afternoon air. I worried about being accused of a crime
I didn't commit, switched evidence.

It was a suburban neighborhood of abrupt boys
running, stopwatches, athletic accidents, stitches,

snuck cigarettes, stashed girlie magazines, pogo sticks,
headlocks, handlebars to fall from. Bikes to balance on

the back of while the rider rode standing. I knew nothing
about how any of it worked, paychecks, much less wills?

I thought if a man and woman slept back to back,
that produced a baby.

So I worried about bunking up with my brother on vacations.
I worried we'd somehow without our knowing

be some taboo bride and groom. I thought sex might involve
the belly button, no—maybe, maybe—you drank something,

a guy's urine? My not-knowing showed itself walking to school—
when girls from blocks over would stop for me, remind me,

you know nothing.
I knew nothing about the origin of the creek,

what to do forgotten at the frozen pond,
evidenced by my walking home

two miles in my ice skates,
only to get in trouble for dulling the blades.

I knew nothing about traveling fathers, sad oblivious
mothers, wasp nests in sheds, how to pay attention,

little experiments with fire, how to inhale, why,
why people moved, were quiet or not,

pleased or explosive, math, foreign languages, good
and evil, cause and effect. It all always seemed so arbitrary.

I jumped from the high bars, and my knee hit my chin,
and my teeth went through my tongue.

Like time-lapse photography, I was healed in two days.
Bats circled at night when we jumped

from swings in the trees.
Most days we built dams on the outskirts,

moved rocks, rerouted water, made pools, so pleased with
the splicing, forking, all the effort and strategy, sliding

eventually into sleep like otters off glossy rocks.
The Russians were racing us to the moon.

Tangled in blankets, I fell out of bed and broke
my collarbone—tangled in blankets,

I screamed myself awake from dreams immediately forgotten
to watch Late-Night with my father smoking and drinking in the living room.

I knew nothing about bras, thought breasts conical
and hard like those of statues.

I didn't know how to do reading problems,
simple distance and time, calculate—join the girl scouts,

get beyond a simple stitch, match plaids in sewing class.
I didn't know about Saturdays when my father would use a haircut

as his excuse to swing by a bar before noon;
I just knew I'd end up there in that basement bar

downtown again. My brother singing while I did the twist
in my plaid wool skirt to twist later on the stool

with my Shirley Temple to twist dutifully
into the house sideways shimmying past my mother.

I carried a bag from the hardware store. As if
that was why we went out!

He pretended he needed a few nails,
handful of odd screws, maybe a can of turpentine.

I'd slide through the small space first—between my mother
holding the door and the doorjamb.

My mother's full lips a hard line.
Coming over the lawn,
my father and brother laughing.

VISITING

Back to the elderly relatives our father took us—
Betty Wherry, retired assistant to Senator Smith,
who lived for years in DC, then with her ancient blind mother
at the beach—Uncle Paul and Aunt Minnie, childless in decorum,
insisting we dress for breakfast, had run a travel agency
in Boston for the wealthy when the Victorian trip meant
seeing the world—worldwide arrangements—
Paris, Egypt, Rome, and Hong Kong.

My brother and I, quiet, were afforded freedoms, silent
in our browsing—closets, bedrooms, the shelves beside the fireplace
with museum quality artifacts to indicate a past—having been somewhere.
Always cocktail hour somehow—a cocktail hour
that sailed surely right over dusk, dinner was just crackers
topped with the cursive of Cheez Whiz.

Silent, in my respectful good behavior, I paid attention—
the blind look that indicated elderly listening—the thin braceleted arms
parceling out the peanuts, refilling the glass companionably
with the warm ginger ale—the speckled hands—the occasional Band-Aid—
contusions purple-pretty under the thin skin—the speckled necks—
the birdie ankles—the eyeglasses and the canes.
How could one live on the coast and not go in?
Why—why . . . the beach but not the beach?
The surf too rough to chance—the uneven bottom—
invisible riptide.

Eventually standing up to my narrow hips in soupy clots of seaweed,
stomach slapped by each impossibly bitter wave, I knew—
I knew my body—knew my body would surely
never, never be theirs.

LOCATION, LOCATION

The photographs came out of the bottom drawer
of my grandmother's secretary—sea captain reclined with watermelon,
spinster sisters in a meadow, Uncle Charles (who ran the brothel)
on the shore road, not much more.

Great-grandmother came from Norway to die in an evening gown,
splayed on the windshield, returning to Woods Hole from
a fundraising to-do in Boston. All that's visible in the small circle
of light thrown on the never-thought-of ancestry.

*The landscape derived from upland glacial deposit coastal bluff
formed with retreat. Sailors approaching and looking westward
at the bluffs saw a long stretch of unvegetated banks that
mariners referred to as the tablelands of the Cape.*

Historical, ancient—estuaries, bays, and marshes
separate land from sea. Spits and islands,
tidal inlets shift with the continual interplay
of ground, sea, breaking waves,
prevailing wind, shoaling.

THIS

The nurse blamed me as the elevator doors began to close—
she pointed when she saw me—said something about
how relieved she was that family had finally shown up—finally—

we hardly looked like family—Jimmy was skimming
and Ed had a flask and a briefcase—we looked like the mob.
I had come to the hospital to visit my father—the spectacular drinker—

I was sixteen—beautiful—because of my lazy sadness
and lack of self-awareness—there between the two cronies
as the elevator was about to go down—
the nurse had been on the previous day evidently—three to eleven—

and in that moment as Jimmy the embezzler held the doors
for her as she explained—claimed my father was just lonely—
only thing wrong with him was he needed someone
to talk with—why wouldn't I talk with him?

She was middle-aged with a flushed puffy face—
a large pleasing mouth—head of auburn curls—
pretty in a sleepy overworked kind of way.
She admitted staying after her shift was over to keep him company—
I might have laughed—how many of my teachers, random
secretaries in offices?

He was a con so steeped in his own longing he turned
like cider to a brilliant long pour—no one would have taken him
for the womanizer he was—and that was the fire of it—
just the right amount of self-regard—humility—self-interest

and empathy—story—silence—not a looker—
not handsome exactly but certainly looking.

He was forty-six and dying—although
we didn't know that yet. Just moments before he had written
his last check—the last check in the checkbook and he went on about that—
the irony—last check—empty account.

He chuckled—pleased—that he actually had the fifteen dollars
for the phone in the room.

Great, I had said—my enthusiasm expansive and sarcastic—
as he handed me the empty checkbook—he had great handwriting.
I watched pleased as he signed year in and year out
all my report cards at the kitchen table—bright morning—
smell of eggs. My pretty mother in her bathrobe.
He'd hold the pen and pause a moment before he wrote—
do a little circle just above the paper before he claimed his name.

Drunks don't start out that way.

That afternoon he was full of the usual—the suicide talk—
the world would do better without him—wasn't he too much trouble?
He was better dead than alive—at least there was insurance—
he acted like I'd be an heiress—*an heiress without lunch money*
was what I thought. I was just glad he was in bed—good as roped down—
not careening up and down the East Coast in his Oldsmobile,
not killing anyone.

That afternoon he was talking ghosts in the hallway—
long-dead relatives arguing—he'd lost forty pounds in a week—
not a gray hair on his head.

I was not thinking he was dying then—
I was so used to his flamboyant dying—falling down stairs,
embarrassing me with the bar room talk before my friends—
claiming him in emergency rooms.

Here's the thing—he was so afraid of dying he wanted it over with.

The nurse pointed to me just before the doors of the elevator closed.
Jimmy held the doors apart—just long enough for the crazy nurse
to point at me and say—wildly—that this—this—

this—was all my fault.

THE ACCOUNTING

Of course, there is some sort of accounting,
right as you leave this world—stepping down

the rocky embankment, a purgatory.
Birdsong, hoof clatter, shadows and dark silhouettes
through the branches,

puddles of sunlight. The almost seen
is what we face—leaving our bodies.

What we rationalized for years, fleetingly, seemed
the crime that no one person would ever be blamed for.
Weren't we collectively responsible?

So, so . . . it is odd, leaving this world to feel so singled out.
But there—quickly—every species that has vanished

is what each of us faces in vanishing.

THAT FEELING

So much of driving, unconscious really,
the familiar route past the cluster of houses—the empty church

and on past the nursery, spring shrubs and window boxes—
a parking lot so jammed with optimism they need a cop for the pull out.

Of course, on the long trips, excursions, we've got both hands on the
    wheel—
GPS, satellite bounce back—all and all—it's living consciously—
doing one's best—feeling plugged in.

So when she hits the blinker on the highway
and checks her rearview mirror
and side mirror and even turns around, she misses that other car
in that extended moment traveling the same speed miraculously—

just behind her right ear—a flourish of hair—glare,
not night—or winter or particularly busy as she moves from the passing

lane to the right—to slow down and cruise—
no one else around—so that the way she is graced in a blaring

extenuated horn of near-miss fatality loosens her heart—
makes her feel apologetic to the very ground.

The other driver curses dramatically with all the hand motions going—
going and gone—she feels like an elderly speedster
in his backsplash—not that she's elderly or speeding or
wearing those extreme sunglasses with the peripheral glare protection,

but that is exactly what it feels like for a second as she swears off driving—
apologizes—shaken to some higher power of the nine lives of cats—rattled.

So glad she didn't kill anyone in that moment.
It is deep embarrassment she feels—true

incompetent not-deserving-to-be-on-the-literal-road shame—
just as one standing in the supermarket checkout must feel,
with the deflated canvas grocery bags,

about the news of the sperm whale off Spain with
sixty-four pounds of trash in its digestive track,
ropes, trash bags, plastic nets—*netting*.

FROM THE ROAD WALKING

From the road walking that window is a dim amber
suggesting the cold and complicated Bruegel village.

Those Dutch knew the certainty of table and appetite—
the subtle shallow puddle of luminosity names each plate.

There's fruit companionable in a bowl—
a pewter pitcher pitched on the stack of neglected reading

beside the book—the *History of Art*—and beside that—
a pile of complicated linen, but that's later—for now, the sudden rain

has retreated, blown to the side—so the sunlight shafting into the sea
blows open the end of the day. The wind tosses the few boats darkly

as if painted there—green chop, leaf toss—wind stream—
horns through the tallest trees—makes us want to run openmouthed

as children spinning. In the tallest story—all end-of-the-day light—
angling gold—direct as good scotch, brightens in

the momentary leafing of those leaves gilded—flaring bronze—highlight—
against the middle ground—dark wood—ruddy hillside that we climb.

Momentarily—one might believe that all this might just be survivable.
Look—at the little harbor, the day tiny and strung up tidy as a hare!

In this light we're aware of background and foreground, what shrinks—
what's provisional—the space we share—and we don't care—

might feel—like nothing bad—nothing bad—
will ever happen to any one of us.

***

THE CISTERN

After the water running between the fingers
of the cupped hands, every bowl in a way
a boast concerning containment.
It is a stone font—impressive as the wheel.
The water clear, and the chill drawn up
from the rock beneath us,
the chill wicked up like the moon
over the green hill, the surprise of rock
and orbit chalky white in the dark blue sky.
Slip your hand in to remind yourself
of the pattering rain, the cycle
of cloud, river, and mist.
Remember the horse
that lowers its head to drink.
Acquiesce—dunk your entire head into that
outdoor sink just for the shock and stagger—
the astonishing cold. Then, lie on the stone walk
to burn like a secret
under the silence of the sun.

FLAMES BEHIND YOUR HEAD

This is where the bees and wasps spiral.
Is it possible this field is forgotten,
that no one has pruned these fruit trees
in fifty years? The old pear trees are too tall
for any ladder, the gesture of scraggly limbs
gorgeous against the height of storm clouds
metaling the distance.
There are the white blossoms that open
the sky like rain in September,
softening like all those returnings—
to school, to home, to evening, to the falling
backward, murmuring green to brown—lost to
sleep in the deep humming collapse of grass.

CARAVAGGIO'S *THE CALLING OF ST. MATTHEW*

At first glance, the stranger and his companion
approaching the table of the tax collector and gamblers
are not recognizable. The two strangers seem
to be lost travelers come to ask a question.
A wood table, coins to indicate a past,
the three roughneck acquaintances
dressed ridiculously to the nines,
buttoned and hooked in bright velvet,
and then our ordinary man, unlikely
in every regard.

Because the background is just a simple Roman tavern wall,
stationed to this world by a window, the panes
covered with oiled paper—we might
call this believable, modern, realistic.

Only a few ways to describe what actually happened—
Matthew touches his chest, indicating a confusion
with this unlikely enlistment.
His companions slouch, dumbfounded amid
the flush and feathers and swords.
There is the humble disbelief
all who are chosen share—that moment
when the world seems just a pile of hammers,
hatchets, buckets of coins—
one thinks plainly *how unlikely*,
absolved from all that is ordinary.

THE ROUND-UP

What happened—old as the hills, ancient as the ax,
the horse, water in a clay cup, dirt under the fingernails.

The river forgets the fish, and the winter sun slides beyond
the far hills. All of them had mothers, and all the mothers sang

as the birds left the trees that ringed the water for the clouds
where the distance whispered a different dream than

the dream dreaming this dark afternoon. The men were boys
not that long ago—delicate, confident, paddling

alongside their mothers through the hot afternoons.
The water dark green with splash and shout—

summer just a whistle and gone. Of course, the night will still hold
stars, the moon's journey, the planet's orbit. There will always be

nests, branches, the swaying and the saying. They all had names
and are men exactly like you, lined up in jackets, boots, and caps—
cold with the waiting.

Trucked out to nowhere are doctors, lawyers, plumbers,
builders, bankers. It is winter, snow rides the collapse of clouds.

There are just shades of brown and gray, a line of trees—
a dark scribble like the markings done by a child.

As each man is shot, whether he drops backward
or to the side, he forgets us, his own name,
this place, civilization like a kiss

his intent was to swear return
in the evening at the lit threshold.

SEEN FROM FAR AWAY

Like looking through binoculars there is that strange equation
of sight and distance when you notice the angel riding
a bicycle through the snowy streets.

On the hem of his garment are a few stains
from his parents' lovemaking. Nothing flashy—just
a faint discoloring of white fabric, which by the time

he reaches the brick school will look just like the after-mark
of melting snow. He has a couple candles for his mother
stashed in a pants pocket, which makes the riding more difficult.

He thinks of the leg motion the way one thinks of opposites—
remembers health when ill, longs for summer during winter.
He is careful not to let the dress tangle in the bicycle gears.

He is always conscious that life is a story.
Often, the narrator is an imaginary sports announcer—
prone to fits of generosity.

The day is just the double-edged horizon with sleep
on either line in the distance. He thinks of the phrase
let something happen,

and it means something different than it used to.
He used to think of a particular girl who served food
in the cafeteria letting something happen—a long line of buttons

tracing her backbone, a winter moon shimmering
above a hill, and in a dream he can't decipher snow drifting
silently into his mouth, and bells from a distant mosque

tangle in her hair. The fantasy was about her recognizing him.
He wanted to be noticed, singled out from the hundreds of boys
seated at the long tables under the high windows

under the enormous ceiling in the bright gash of light
and noontime rough housing. He used to anticipate her
walking back and forth, stacking the trays, replacing

the napkins near his table. She wore a white uniform,
apron, hairnet that contained the massive coil of dark hair
brushed up, revealing the nape of neck as she looked down,

concentrating . . . spoons, forks, knives. An angel
attracting no attention—a boy on the way to a theater.
Wings—appearing unlikely as the type that actually work—

lift the boy riding a rusted ten-speed
through the slush of the ancient, darkened city,
pushed by the palm of wind.

Just as sunlight will always name each tree, he knows
not much will ever change—soldiers are still taking families out
in the hush of the forest, positioning groups in front of the trenches

as if it were a photo they were after. It is like looking through
the wrong end of a telescope—seeing the soldiers positioning
the people in front of the trenches in the silence of a drawn breath.

Even at this great distance you are able to count silently all the trees
there are hundreds. I wonder how many shovels it takes?
Look at the wool coats, the black freckles' random design

splattered across the white birch bark, the length of the shadow
falling off the many trees digging the distance. The shadows there
weigh as much as pianos. No music, no voice,

it is the same ancient moon pearled,
flushed, rising out of the heights of bare,
knuckled branches, that illuminates the cool,
turned cheek of a soldier, turning.

THE CLOSE OF WINTER

(mass grave near the town of Abda, Hungary, 1946)

There is only the road away.
She wanders the day feeling singled out.

Odd reversal—thinking, *I am surprised that I live.*
Black streets, gray roofs, posed trees.

Imagine, digging up the body!
A woman pawing a body out of the wet mud.

The corpse discovered no more resembles her husband's
live body than a suit animates a man. The body

she searched for, sprawled with the other open mouths,
weird gestures, and fixed glances, is not

anything she has known.

Sliding down into the grave the sky is ragged,
something torn. The spring light trembles and weeps.

His body, the key to tumble the lock—the not-knowing,
the muddy field. The wind gains speed, opens the emptiness.

She looks at the landscape and is undone by the trees
dreaming their old dreams of green leaves.

Basically, nothing in those pockets, no note, not even
his hands held up before his face, poker face,
that unconscious gesture. Those hands before that face,

trying to halt the years,
empty and wet like carts pulled by the dumb gray donkeys.
The years moving without him through the dark,
through the feathered, notwithstanding trees
like empty carts pulled.

Like a song she cannot forget, the grave, the body,
everywhere—anywhere—so that the whole landscape shovels itself
into just a place to throw the bodies.

DEPTH OF FIELD: BRUEGEL'S *HUNTERS IN THE SNOW*

Think of the insane, those puzzles of foreground
and background—what one normally sees,
is supposed to see. There is the bright even wash
of illumination making each little root,
each brown leaf curl, detail . . . spring forward, distinct.

For weeks before this, just the huge hollow
blow of the wind, enormous in its passage,
making everyone feel small, dwarfed.
The dark trees encircling the hamlet,
a scrimshaw etched against the snowy sky.

To be one of the returning—
leaving the stenciled deep woods!
Coming back, the hunters stomp up
the white hill above the village, see the frozen ponds,
the cluster of barns and homesteads.
If it had only been a painting, a dark bird
would drift, some cold current dedicating the eye
to the peaks of background.

One realizes it took years to perfect this: seeing the way we see—
being able to distinguish the tree line *and* the deer,
his rack which is not the smoke of branches stacked up
behind him. The sun simply a halo
in just another predictable Dutch sky.

BLACK BOUGH

> *Truth*:
> to know ourselves,
>   *from the beginning,*
>   *hung.*
>
> —Octavio Paz

The bright light tightens
around a few scrawny trees, a lone loitering dog.

No help comes.
Imagine staring into the sun, then
how the clouds spread out and open like wallets
over a few corrugated roofs.

Anyone being taken to his execution
would finger that well-polished stone of a story—
Dostoyevsky, the cruel joke when the prison guards faked
the firing squad, down to lining up the condemned,
tying the blindfolds, positioning the prisoners against
the dappled stone wall in the frozen courtyard.

Anyone being taken to his execution would imagine Fyodor Dostoevsky
packed off to Siberia in the rattle of the farce, especially
if the papers for his hanging weren't in order in the morning.

There is a formality to our lack of attention.
It is raining in London, sunny in Boston,
overcast in Brussels, and the guards play cards in a trance
in the stilled hot courtyard.

A small outdoor square, vinyl kitchen chairs,
bottles of soda, and the drifting swagger of a pop tune.

There is a small square to stand on.
But then the step is kicked away—

The only chore some have to do before lunch
is throw a dead weight onto the back bed of a truck
and cover it with a tarp. After eating, they drive,
the leaves shine, and damp undergrowth holds
the shifty shadows like a dark reserve. The wind staggers,

the ground flinches, the anonymous sun floods
the clearing with free admission, allowing anything to grow.

Later, there is the dusty truck, an oil drum,
the men impersonating soldiers lock up the door
to a hard-to-find place.

* * *

EVENING SONG

The daylilies wince shut, reduced to orange tongues
waving by the woodshed, woozy on the wind.

My neighbors, the brothers, wait near the river
for the black snake. Wearing gloves, sitting by the stone wall,

they watch the rubble where the snake last disappeared,
quick as a needle pulling thread. The men trap catfish, eels,

crabs. Eventually, dusk subtracts, each small fishing boat
moored and the clouds anchored by tall trees. The brothers talk

and watch the sky and river couple—fall darkly into each other.
If the snake appeared now, no one could pick it out. This is a game

they won't likely win as the muskrat swims back and forth, carrying
small clumps of river silt in her mouth toward a nest in the rocks.

The muskrat is diligent as the darkness, which plows over everything,
burying us in its furrow. I am only a woman on a nearby pier

holding a pair of muddy gardening gloves, momentarily stopped,
listening to the ducks squabbling and shuffling in the shallows

as the day is pulled out. It happens in a moment, seemingly—
dusk to dark. I can't help but imagine the large dark clipper sweeping by,

the ancient prow curling the water to
a bright lip, running out—the obliteration is only,
only a shadow cast over us with each swift pass.

FROM ANOTHER PAST, *THIS PAST*

From there, it could have been any town
anchored off that pre-revolutionary harbor.
A stone bridge dotted with light, occasional birds
emerging through ancient sounds, loud and throaty,
to skim the surface. A confusion with the wind and tide,
each going the opposite direction, made the boat spin.
That is what woke us, that going around.

There were stars, tentative as all those guttering candles.
That was when I realized, looking to the sky,
that it was just the current, tide and wind—
meeting each other like magnets of equal strength.

We have forgotten how
to make the things we need, and
everything comes from too far away.

ANOTHER REPUBLIC

For Katherine

When we come upon the hawk for the first time,
I am reminded of the line by Cézanne,
the landscape thinks itself in me,

then imagine a current of sunlight for the bird,
the aerial pencil sketch of nearby meadows
and woods, the light hysterical.

My neighbor caught the red-tailed hawk with a gloved hand
when the bird spun into his workshop, all confused flight,
feathers to wall, stunning itself against a windowpane.

Talon, beak, square white breast dappled brown, big as a cat.
Called to come see this wild thing, anyone would think
of hunger and the imperceptible movement in the grass.

All the neighborhood children are in a circle
surrounding the cage when I leave.
There is a branch, a swatch of old carpet,

a towel covering the set-up. I tell my daughter
to walk straight home after the bird is fed, tagged, and released.
The trees are leafless, married to rivers of damp shadow.

The sky is that diluted blue
that accompanies bright light, reminiscent of when
the water colorist drenches the sheet and blue blurs

by degrees to white. Dense old growth dwarfs
the spackle of the short ornamental flowering trees.
I think of the bed of feathers, twirled reeds,

the perch and vision afforded by the swaying
upper story of the tallest trees. A while later I see
my little girl running, big coat unbuttoned, open,

flying toward home. Entering the kitchen
she is out of breath, reports all that was left
in the end was the fat little gerbil's head,

the little gold seeds from its belly.
She walks with purpose toward the black piano,
throws the red coat to the floor, and plays

the classical solos memorized till there is a space,
a blue square of sky between herself and
the awful order of things, what is devoured,

the gloved hand, the hooded eye, the bird's hunger.
The music is a curtained window that contains
the great beyond, and she plays like

a dog runs—it doesn't know what it is doing,
but it equals distance.

DO YOU BELIEVE IN THE AFTERLIFE?

It has nothing to do with loving this life,
was what he said. It was evening.
The problem was time, its tyranny, a dogged refusal
to be revisited. When she thought about the past
she thought it miserly. *You know*, he said,
how last night we stood here?
The bargain was suddenly clear to her.
Living in the country, the great spaces
between the houses. The river just a black line
that underscored the sky.

The dim gold light, snow rising outside,
the river stiffening and growing hard.
She knew the look he gave her, his answer
had something to do with the people he had loved
and lost, their stone faces, closed eyes
and folded hands. The answer had something to do
with the cold, millions of black branches,
the great Russian novels open on his chest, youth,
sleeping in the single bed, the long apartment
in the large city of the past, the Italians upstairs
cooking, his aunt and mother, silent,
walking the halls of before, putting away
the white dishes and folded clothes, sleep coming
steadily as rain, the darkened windows.

TRAINING

A simple pedestrian loneliness rode me.
I felt it between the shoulder blades, clamped
to the nape of my neck, taking the evening train south
past all those boarded-up storefronts, narrow,
cluttered backyards. My face floating
on the surface of the window; three views—
the rush of evening outside, my own pale ghost,
then, the strangers behind me dozing or talking
and drinking in the lit interior of the club car.

Shutter flash, bushes, damp trees,
backs of houses no one is supposed to see, piles of stuff,
and a river finally with hardly more than just a trace
of reflected light. Lining the water, the festively lit boathouses
along the Schuylkill River that brought to mind all those men
that Eakins painted—sculling. Or Gustave Caillebotte's
The Floor Scrapers. All that ropey effort!
Before I knew it we were out in the country, passing
fields, miles of trees, then the small inlets
of the upper Chesapeake Bay.

We've slowed down for a switch,
and on a lit porch a woman shakes out a tablecloth
and is gone. If she glanced toward the train,
I wondered if she saw me—momentarily,
girlish with regret, suddenly knowing,
no matter how old you are
sometimes, the ultimate dark deception—
going home.

THE KITCHEN

Sunday afternoon and I was undone,
the way I always was by another week beginning.
It's the old lament of any child on Sunday, dreading Monday.
Walking back up the gravel drive, hands shoved in my pockets,
nothing on my mind but peeling carrots, my daughter's new piano,
and the chance of fitting it through the narrow doorway.

It would not have surprised me if Dürer's *Four Horsemen of the Apocalypse*
charged right though the hedge where the autumn leaves had blown
against the dark trunks and tunnels of shadow. Wet, windy ground,
the muck and overflow that equaled spring, so bright
one had to look down.

My daughter was off with her friend, the little girl—
her hostage, mate, princess. Those two reminded me of how little
was needed—a necklace, scarf, and a couple of stones.
That was when he pushed up against me, and we stripped
all our clothes in the kitchen.
In the afternoon light, in the bluntness of our desire
after years, we fumbled like animals.

THE DREAM

Everything in abundance, the light seems to whisper
to the pale grass again and again. What would it be
like to be an animal grazing? The dream begins
with a question. The light pushing everything
into position on that distant border from
where the rain eventually comes. Because
in dreams nothing need make sense—
this is a landscape before time. It is a world
of hunger, where movement and time hang on
being satisfied—sufficient water.
Imagine—the twisted tree with the large boughs
for lounging cats, above
the birds scattering—
the landslide of hunger
that moves the lion forward.
For a moment, I am just the beating heart, spliced
separate from the gazelle's rising and falling chest,
crimson under the blue sky stopping.

DIVORCE

Like a high school girl, I proposed splitting up
with a note—concluding with the promised intention
we'd certainly get back together.
There was marriage counseling I dutifully thoroughly lied through.
I sat off to the side like a middle-aged woman kitting
through the theater, zoning meetings with my bag of wool,
a library book or two, extra needles at her feet.

By then, I knew exactly what was elaborately wrong with him.
That year, I was purposeful, moving with
a sort of industrial efficiency
toward no end in my blazer and button-down,
buttery leather purse slung across my chest.
I knew how to talk about it—except, I had no idea.

I moved to a big old house, a three story—
that needed to have its guts ripped out—
the knob and tube, galvanized plumbing, gas line
from the street dug up, water line from the street dug up,
not to mention the whole old world replaster,
then, kitchen, something done with the elm.

I slept in a big old coat without dreaming
on the chaise lounge in the snow in the outback.

∗ ∗ ∗

NOVEMBER

Practically every child knows there is just as much tree
underground as above. The intricate roots branching below
the surface to match that upper story tossing its canopy.

Autumn began in the stormy brightness of leaf fall,
windy plunder, like a plainsong at dusk or
deer grazing slowly, and this tree seems
light-headed, singing that song, flaring
orange and burnt red, over-the-top, going
loudly toward the full-frontal abandon
of bare facades and darkened storefronts,
the empty shelves of winter,
ramshackle winter
to arrive at the reverse silhouette.
The stripped tree, mirror image reflected
at every lake's shore.

How I envy the way the tree interrupts
itself each year to seemingly snap shut,
stand bare. It's enviable, the way the tree loses
its dream-flared crown, seed blown
somersault breaking with birds
as the world goes cold and clear.

THE STARFISH

The tide comes in
and with each grizzly crest everything below vanishes.
Then, a moment later the shallows are hyper-clear;
the small shells, pebbles, bedraggle of seaweed sway in the lurch.
The sunken suspension clatters like costume jewelry
in some drawer pulled out too fast.

It's befitting my style that I don't know
what it is I've come to find.
A true beachcomber, head down,
slow and clandestine—the bright pools, polished
rock, slick steps. The lesson everywhere—
that water finds its way; water's way is to find its way—
under the wind's vagrant path.

The water is mercurial cold, the opening to
the rocky crevice so like a stokehole to an old furnace.
This is the rudimentary world—
crustacean, barnacle, the submerged,
stepping-stones magnified under
the tide's biting trace.

THE WOMEN'S PRISON

Driving out there one can pretend one is going
to the sea, the same sort of two-lane roads,
old-fashioned vegetable and plant stands,
gritty truck plazas, gravel turnarounds.

Low scrub pine, an occasional ruined Victorian set far back
from the sandy shoulder of the road.
I go in empty-handed and know
I've never been as empty-handed in this life.

The prison book club is waiting for me,
I feel it signing in, handing over my license, clipping
my photo badge to my collar, waiting for the door
to unlock after I've been frisked. I feel their patience
as I pause for the metal door to slide open, as
I proceed under the guard tower,
circles and circles of razor wire along
the electrified fences. I feel them waiting for me
at countless doors, going through a series of low
nondescript buildings. I walk to the next desk and sign in,
see the bulletproof glass and, hanging on a peg board,
hundreds of various-sized handcuffs and assorted riot gear.

This isn't like television.
There is a ceremony in the gym
reminiscent of the impoverished church social.
Relatives and children visiting, it was hard to witness.
The library isn't really a library, reminds me

of a Sunday school classroom with its linoleum, out-of-date
women's magazines, round tables and easy readers,
inspirational posters. There are books, but the books are not
real literature, the sort of thing that can save one's life.

The women are wearing men's jumpsuits and sweats.
As I take off my jacket and pass out the poems I've copied,
I imagine briefly *being defined completely
by my mistakes.*

THE GREYHOUND

The greyhound was black with a white patch
on her chest, white streak accentuating the long nose.
A slow walker, head down, dramatic in exasperation,
plopping down every couple blocks to rest
on various lawns. She was stubborn, had her own
elaborate ideas, favorite routes. She liked
the back alley, favored Newland Road, Canterbury.
Could do without going down Suffolk or
Southway. The irony, she was a slow rambler,
and one received pleased attention or huffy dismissal,
it just depended. Often, she was busy nursing
a mysterious grudge.

My neighbor, yes, a little bird of a woman,
adopted the greyhound because it had blown its leg.
When faced with the choice between three
ex-racers, a friend encouraged her to
"take the crippled one."
My neighbor had a cane, a hip replaced.
In a baggy black wool coat, red baseball cap,
she walked far, late nights in every sort of weather.

The tiny skinny woman, the big skinny dog both
limped until they didn't anymore.

At the monastery, that dog could finally do the open hills.
Once, she chased a buck with a full rack till he turned
and thought, "who, who the hell?"
The dog was close enough to lick his haunch.

Often, she simply sat at the rise and scanning,
scanning the distance for the smallest movement,
her attention absolutely otherworldly.
There was something about that,
that patience and confidence and launch,
that made us do some research,
look the dog up by her numbers.

Low and behold she had been the queen
of the Florida racetracks, five years running,
she had been the four-million-dollar dog.
The joy was in the launch,
the hair-fine moment, the running—
a sort of spiritual integration that even
the most distracted of us somehow recognized.

I buried a lot of her loot: the badger (of which
she was particularly proud), various rabbits,
the impressively heavy groundhog.
Sometimes the greyhound streaked down
the street if she noticed me opening up my car.
I'd find her composed and sitting in the back seat
staring straight ahead through the windshield
before I even knew she'd somehow arrived.

WHAT WE NEED

What we need is the red barn,
the low treeless hills that frame
the two big ponds, the moon that seems to see
the barn roof as something to rise above.
But before that happens, deer
like dusk come down from those slight hills,
slow and hungry. If we were thinking,
we would say dusk is the ultimate consumptive.

Like most beauty—
the deer arrive unnoticed and then,
simply, are indisputable.
One looks up and the light is going.

Dug in beside the pond is an old apple tree
that drops an apple every evening.
That's the action and, whether we are here
or not, it would make a sound.

Dragonflies and butterflies had stitched
the ragged edge of the water during the hot
afternoon, but now it is quiet, darker,
as bats reel out from the rafters.

We drag the chairs out to sit beside the pond
and watch the tree while the dogs wander.
Sometimes in the bronze light at the end of the day,
they chase a lone car. We can go off too far
in the woods mid-morning.

There are interludes:
a huge snapping turtle, a skunk,
then dramatically—a porcupine.

The dogs are simply and utterly *game*
in a way we still have time to learn.
What we need is to learn to be—
curious, interested without being
interesting. When the dogs are bored
they are like young boys—pawing,
prodding—all mouth-to-mouth without bite,
paws scrabbling and rolling without
the knowledge of not quite where.

The truth is, the hounds, like most of us,
are better together than alone, smarter together
than one alone. We watch the dogs,
jaunty and optimistic, going on their way.
Their investigations begin at the shadows
where Schumacher Road meets with
Stony Lonesome in the wet low
lands and floral ditches.

THE STAND-IN

It's almost too late when the bulbs go in the ground.
The garden hardly indistinguishable from the strewn ruin
everywhere. Still, there is the faint edge if one looks close enough—
a soft trench under the creeping weeds evident where
the yard begins and garden ends. I'm told it is reminiscent
"of a wall dusted away with a brush at an archeological dig."
The nine-year-old boy from across the street helps—talks,
wielding the shovel in the mess of splayed weeds,
dry stems, leggy grass.

There are liberties over here he's not allowed at home.
It started with playing store, included an elaborate setup
(real canned vegetables, limes, boxes of macaroni).
He was the benevolent storekeeper, and I was to play
the desperate customer out of everything.
It evolved then to the use of a permanent marker pricing
groceries (don't ask!) and waterfalls with the hose,
real water and bricks and overflow.

I'm usually in his sights
from his dining room window across the street.
His aunt lives in another state and his grandmother
is increasingly forgetful so I'm glad to oblige. Still,
after all these years, daily visits—arriving immediately
upon return from school, camp, or errands, he pauses
to ask permission to come in, yells my name
through the mail slot.

It's Saturday, late afternoon
with searing light,
plunge of shadow, terrific wind, we work
companionably with our cold hands.

LOVE

I held my wrists out
in surrender—

stepped down into
the subtleties of touch; and with that
came a mysterious detachment.
Nothing moved, really,
because I was in the present tense,
no horizon—just seamless unparalleled
achievement.

If I didn't know better, I'd say those waves
in the distance, those white drifts, were dunes
on the other side of the sea.

DRIVING IN SPRING

As if that flock of starlings rising above the road
in the flourish were single-minded,
that intricate mundane splendor migrating
up and back, down and over above the shorn fields.
The orchard is flung against the hill. Like a curtain
of fish in a school, the tiny birds part, fall and
recover, churn and stir the composure of
the close-cropped farmyard.
It is as if those dark birds were combing the air
with irrelevant syntax, poised to slip through.

There are cold shadows, a yellow farmhouse, struck trees,
everything and nothing to pass.

Maybe I see all of this only because the small black birds
seem to be phrasing the air, flying sideways,
swelling to crescendo, just pattern,
magnetic—reminding anyone here of
that pulling apart and forcing back—
a sash coming undone, the silk robe of the sky
falling open.

Together the birds are an arrow, a warning midair,
everything unraveled, loosened—horses by the fence,
hills blushing in the flash and
alternate glare of cloud and sun.
Those starlings flipping through
shapes are a black breach—are a signal,
a trick with a mirror.

I want to say they signal the thaw,
the branding spring light,
give us thick, ancient scrolls of light
to unravel at the silver leaves,
the black trunks where the world is kept.

NOTES

"Location, Location": the third stanza in italics is from the US Geological Survey's Circular 1417, *Coastal Landforms and Processes at the Cape Cod National Seashore, Massachusetts*, by Graham S. Giese, S. Jeffress Williams, and Mark Adams (Reston, VA: US Department of Interior, 2015).

"The Close of Winter": this is dedicated to Stephen Berg, inspired by Miklós Radnóti's *Clouded Sky*, which Stephen cotranslated with Steven Polgar and S. J. Marks (New York: Harper and Row, 1972).

"The Women's Prison": the last line was inspired by a sentence from Lawrence Downes, "I wondered what it would be like to be defined by my own worst sins." From the op-ed "Oedipus Max: Four Nights of Anguish and Applause in Sing Sing" (*New York Times*, November 18, 2008).